D1171147

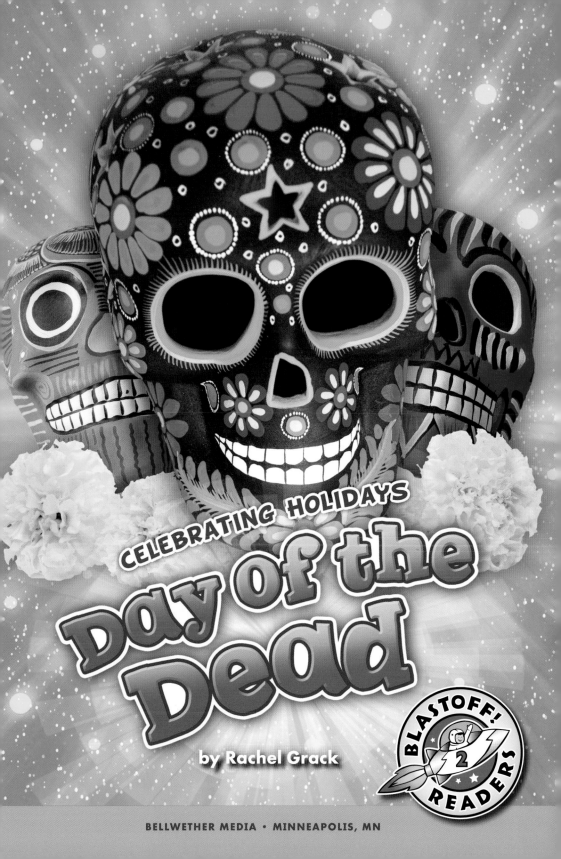

CELEBRATING HOLIDAYS

Day of the Dead

by Rachel Grack

BLASTOFF!
2
READERS

BELLWETHER MEDIA • MINNEAPOLIS, MN

Note to Librarians, Teachers, and Parents:

Blastoff! Readers are carefully developed by literacy experts and combine standards-based content with developmentally appropriate text.

Level 1 provides the most support through repetition of high-frequency words, light text, predictable sentence patterns, and strong visual support.

Level 2 offers early readers a bit more challenge through varied simple sentences, increased text load, and less repetition of high-frequency words.

Level 3 advances early-fluent readers toward fluency through increased text and concept load, less reliance on visuals, longer sentences, and more literary language.

Level 4 builds reading stamina by providing more text per page, increased use of punctuation, greater variation in sentence patterns, and increasingly challenging vocabulary.

Level 5 encourages children to move from "learning to read" to "reading to learn" by providing even more text, varied writing styles, and less familiar topics.

Whichever book is right for your reader, Blastoff! Readers are the perfect books to build confidence and encourage a love of reading that will last a lifetime!

This edition first published in 2018 by Bellwether Media, Inc.

No part of this publication may be reproduced in whole or in part without written permission of the publisher. For information regarding permission, write to Bellwether Media, Inc., Attention: Permissions Department, 5357 Penn Avenue South, Minneapolis, MN 55419.

Library of Congress Cataloging-in-Publication Data

Names: Koestler-Grack, Rachel A., 1973- author.
Title: Day of the Dead / by Rachel Grack.
Description: Minneapolis, MN : Bellwether Media, Inc., 2018. | Series:
   Blastoff! Readers: Celebrating Holidays | Includes bibliographical
   references and index. | Audience: Grades K-3. | Audience: Ages 5-8.
Identifiers: LCCN 2016052738 (print) | LCCN 2017010226 (ebook) | ISBN
   9781626176188 (hardcover : alk. paper) | ISBN 9781681033488 (ebook)
Subjects: LCSH: All Souls' Day–Mexico–Juvenile literature. | Mexico–Social
   life and customs–Juvenile literature.
Classification: LCC GT4995.A4 K64 2017 (print) | LCC GT4995.A4 (ebook) | DDC
   394.266–dc23
LC record available at https://lccn.loc.gov/2016052738

Editor: Christina Leighton   Designer: Lois Stanfield

Printed in the United States of America, North Mankato, MN.

Table of Contents

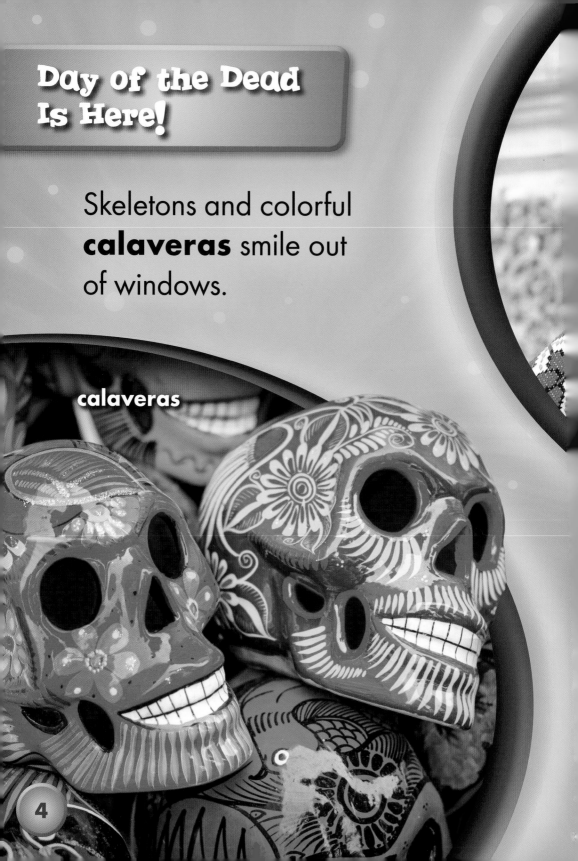

Day of the Dead Is Here!

Skeletons and colorful **calaveras** smile out of windows.

calaveras

People wear face paint.
They play music and
dance in **cemeteries**.
It is Day of the Dead!

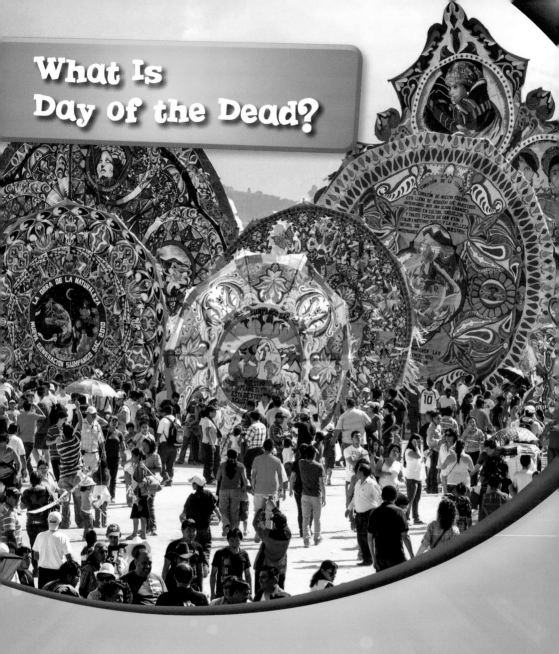

What Is Day of the Dead?

This holiday honors the dead. Families welcome spirits back home.

They celebrate death as a part of life. It is a happy time!

How Do You Say?

Word	Pronunciation
calaveras	CAHL-uh-VARE-ahs
Día de los Muertos	DEE-ah dey lohs MWARE-tohs
ofrendas	oh-FREN-dahs
pan de muerto	PAHN dey MWARE-toh
papel picado	PAH-pel pee-CAH-doh

Who Celebrates Day of the Dead?

Mexico and other parts of **Latin America** celebrate this holiday. They call it *Día de los Muertos.*

Mexico

N
W E
S

The United States also enjoys the holiday.

People in Mexico started to honor the dead thousands of years ago.

They had special
months to remember the
spirits of loved ones.

Today, the holiday combines old **traditions** with All Saints' Day and All Souls' Day.

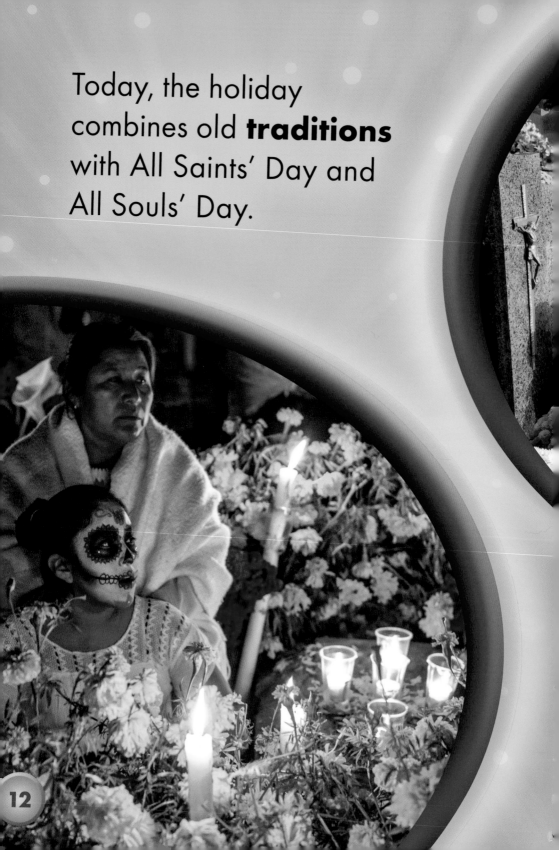

All Saints' Day
in Poland

These **Christian** holidays also
honor the dead.

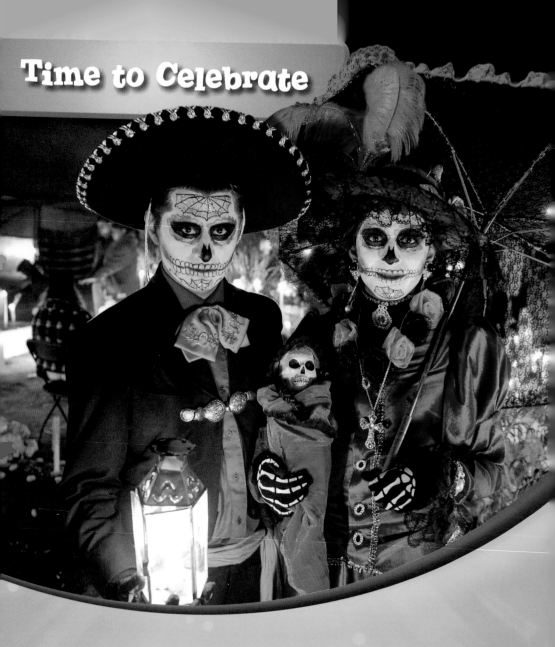

Day of the Dead is on November 2. Children who have died are often remembered the day before.

People clean graves and decorate for the celebrations.

Day of the Dead Traditions!

Ofrendas are important to Day of the Dead. People create **altars** to hold candles, photos, and belongings of the dead.

altar

Make Papel Picado

People decorate altars with *papel picado* (punched paper).

What You Need:
- 4 sheets of colored tissue paper or crepe paper
- pencil or marker
- scissors

What You Do:
1. Cut four different colors of paper into 9-inch by 6-inch rectangles.
2. Fold each sheet in half.
3. Draw designs on all four edges of each folded paper. Leave a space between each shape.
4. Cut out each shape. Unfold the papers to see your designs.

bread of the dead

Families offer water and food
to the spirits. Bread of the dead
is a common offering.

This sweet bread is often decorated with bone shapes. Sugar skulls are also popular.

sugar skull

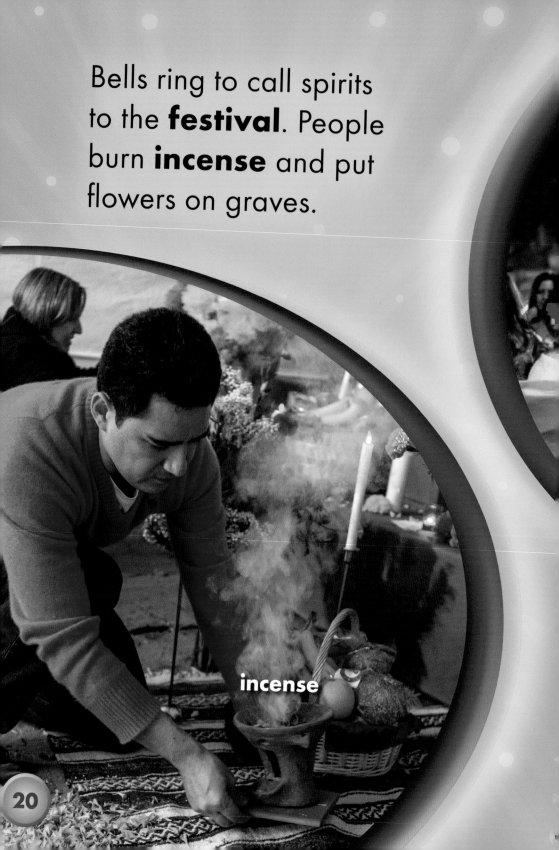

Bells ring to call spirits to the **festival**. People burn **incense** and put flowers on graves.

incense

They are happy to remember the dead!

Glossary

altars—tables set up with offerings that honor people

calaveras—the Spanish word for skulls

cemeteries—places where the dead are buried

Christian—related to Christianity; Christians are people who believe in the teachings of Jesus Christ and the Christian Bible.

festival—a celebration

incense—scented sticks that give off a smell when they burn

Latin America—countries south of the United States where people speak Spanish or Portuguese

ofrendas—the Spanish word for offerings

traditions—customs, ideas, and beliefs handed down from one generation to the next

To Learn More

AT THE LIBRARY
Barner, Bob. *The Day of the Dead: El Día de los Muertos.* New York, N.Y.: Holiday House, 2010.

Hollihan, Kerrie Logan. *Day of the Dead: Día de los Muertos.* New York, N.Y.: Powerkids Press & Editorial Buenas Letras, 2010.

Thong, Roseanne Greenfield. *Día de los Muertos.* Chicago, Ill.: Albert Whitman & Company, 2015.

ON THE WEB
Learning more about
Day of the Dead is as
easy as 1, 2, 3.

1. Go to www.factsurfer.com.

2. Enter "Day of the Dead" into the search box.

3. Click the "Surf" button and you will see a
   list of related web sites.

With factsurfer.com, finding more information is
just a click away.

Index

The images in this book are reproduced through the courtesy of: Judy Bellah/ Alamy, front cover (left and right skulls); Ibeth Ibarra, front cover (center skull); oksana2010, front cover (flowers); Byelikova Oksana, p. 4; Anton_Ivanov, pp. 4-5; robertharding, pp. 6-7; Jesús Eloy Ramos Lara, p. 8; Kobby Dagan, pp. 8-9, 10-11, 12; Tino Soriano/ Getty Images, p. 11; Mirosław Nowaczyk/ Alamy, pp. 12-13; MARIO VAZQUEZ/ Getty Images, pp. 14-15; Philip Mowbray, p. 15; betto rodrigues, p. 16; Lois Stanfield, p. 17 (all); Solange_Z, p. 18 (large); agcuesta, p. 18 (small inset); maogg, p. 19; Ed Lefkowicz/ Alamy, p. 20; Mario Tama/ Getty Images, pp. 20-21; studio BM/ Shutterstock, p. 22.